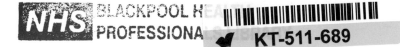

The Blackpool, Fylde & Wyre

Health Li⊦

This book is due for ret··

Books may be ·
Renewals m·

Windmill 2007

THE FUTURE OF HEALTH CARE REFORMS IN ENGLAND

Sarah Harvey, Alasdair Liddell, Laurie McMahon

windmill
2007
SIMULATING HEALTH
FUTURES FOR THE NHS

King's Fund

in partnership with

loop² Monitor
Independent Regulator
of NHS Foundation Trusts
Nuffield Hospitals

Available from:
King's Fund
11–13 Cavendish Square
London W1G 0AN
Tel: 020 7307 2591
Fax: 020 7307 2801

Email: publications@kingsfund.org.uk
www.kingsfund.org.uk/publications

Edited by Caroline Pook
Typeset by Florence Production
Printed in the UK by the King's Fund

Contents

Foreword

Health reform, both in this country and overseas, has long been dogged by the law of unintended consequences. Not only is the service complex, making it difficult to identify appropriate levers of change, but also each part of the system is connected to other parts. Pressure on one component reverberates throughout the system in an unpredictable and varied manner.

It is hardly surprising, then, that as new and different incentives have been introduced in recent years, there has been a growing desire to understand the combined impact of the current health reforms. Along with many others, the King's Fund has researched and evaluated a wide range of policies from the impact of additional funding and the introduction of patient choice, to the effect of Payment by Results and practice-based commissioning. Although this work provides valuable information, more needs to be done to understand the interaction between different initiatives and indeed the nature of the overall system that is being created.

This was apparent in 1990 when the original Rubber Windmill was staged in East Anglia devised by Laurie McMahon, then at the Office for Public Management, and commissioned by Alasdair Liddell, then heading up the East Anglian region of the NHS. That simulation of the then government's attempt to introduce an internal market into the NHS proved to be a powerful learning tool. Some of the lessons were learnt, others were not, but as a participant in that and subsequent events, I became convinced of the insight and learning that such behavioural simulations can provide.

That is why the Fund formed a partnership with Laurie McMahon and Sarah Harvey, from Loop2, Bill Moyes of Monitor and David Mobbs of Nuffield Hospitals to create a new Windmill to help shape our understanding at this critical time in health reform. Alasdair Liddell, now a senior associate at the Fund, acted as the project manager.

This is not a research report – it does not purport to draw together all the available evidence, nor does it profess to be an accurate prediction of the future. The aim is more modest: to assess the strengths and weaknesses in the current levers, explore how they are likely to interact and consider how the system can be made more robust and sustainable going forward.

Windmill 2007 draws on the collective expertise and experience of more than 100 active participants in health care across England – clinicians, managers, policy-makers, regulators and analysts. The project is much more than the two-day simulation of a fictional but realistic health economy from 2008 to 2011 – that was an essential part of the process, but so too were the preparatory meetings to devise the parameters, the debriefing sessions and the subsequent workshops with key players in the system. Every part contributed to the learning.

This report provides valuable insight into how the changes can be made to work effectively and poses questions and challenges for all those who want a health service that is genuinely responsive and effective.

There is one important caveat – the Windmill was conducted in what might be described as a relatively inert political environment. In the simulation, central government offered little obstruction – but neither did they offer much clarity about what they were hoping the system would look like.

We are now at the dawn of a new administration, and our hope is that this Windmill report will provide sufficient 'intellectual currency' to fuel a debate among all those with an interest in health care about how best we can embrace the changes that work, address the areas of weakness and provide a clear vision for the future.

Niall Dickson, Chief Executive, King's Fund
June 2007

Introduction

The Windmill 2007 objectives

Over the past decade the NHS has been subject to successive waves of policy and structural change. The latest iteration, focused mainly on the introduction of market forces into the system, is intended to provoke the most fundamental change to the NHS since its inception. There are radical shifts in the way health needs and demands are managed, in how services are planned and commissioned and in the way that public engagement is organised. We are also seeing huge changes in the range of participants who are able to provide care to NHS patients, in how the system is managed and regulated, and in the funding and resource allocation processes. Given this scale of change, it is not surprising that many clinicians and managers – and, perhaps, members of the public – are having difficulty in understanding how and whether these developments will result in the desired improvements in health outcomes, productivity and responsiveness to patient needs and preferences. A common complaint is that there is no way of working out where all the changes will lead: there is no 'big picture'. This is making managers and decision-makers less certain about where to make their long-term investments and disinvestments.

In order to develop this 'big picture' – to test out and understand where the latest health system reforms (and all the myriad interactions between them) might lead the NHS – the King's Fund, Nuffield Hospitals and Monitor decided to sponsor Windmill 2007, based on a behavioural simulation designed by Loop2. The Windmill name harks back to a much earlier simulation-based project: The Rubber Windmill (which Laurie McMahon and Greg Parston, then at the Office for Public Management, ran for the East Anglian Regional Health Authority in 1990 to explore how the health service was responding to the 'new' internal market). That event produced powerful learning and passed into NHS history. We believe that Windmill 2007 has generated some similarly valuable insights into the health system of the future.

The objectives of Windmill 2007 were to help to understand:

- how the complex array of health system reforms – changes in demand, supply, transaction and management – will interact and what the 'big picture' of health care will be like in the future

- how the various stakeholders involved in the planning, delivery and consumption of health care will react to the changing incentives resulting from patient choice, competition, commissioning, regulation and market management

- 'who has to pull what levers' to ensure that the opportunities of the reforms are fully understood and the potential pitfalls avoided, so that the new system works to deliver real improvements for patients.

The Windmill 2007 design

Windmill 2007 comprised four main elements:

- a workshop on 4 December 2006 involving a number of leading thinkers and commentators across the system, to help to identify the main drivers and tensions to be explored in the simulation event

- the simulation event itself, held on 5–6 March 2007, bringing together nearly 70 participants: policy-makers, regulators, managers and clinicians (from both the NHS and independent sectors)

- a workshop on 1 May 2007 to review and test the emerging findings with those who had been invited to the December workshop

- a stakeholder event on 9 May 2007, involving professional and third sector groups that had not been involved in the previous events, to review and test further the emerging findings.

Each of these elements – and in particular the discussions that took place with those involved before, during and after these events – contributed to the insights and learning that have informed our observations and recommendations in this report. While the core component of the Windmill process was undoubtedly the simulation event, it is important to emphasise that what happened during the 'play' – although highly realistic – was much less important than the insights and learning that emerged from it, moderated by discussion with the participants of all four elements.

For the simulation itself we needed to model a whole system and, in order to make the task manageable, we had to be selective about the main focus of our enquiry. At an early stage, we made a decision not to include mental health and learning disability services. These are hugely important service areas but have somewhat different dynamics to the rest of health care, and to model them effectively would have added to the complexity of the simulation event. We recognised, however, that they would be interesting Windmill topics in their own right.

Part 1: Learning from simulations – the Windmill 2007 design

Why use a behavioural simulation?

The orthodox approach for planners to predict the future is to use historical, quantitative data and – with varying degrees of sophistication – to extrapolate from the current Point A to a Point B on the distant horizon. This may work well for concrete issues in relatively stable environments; however, such an approach offers much less predictive value in circumstances where we are trying to understand the future of complex social systems in more chaotic environments. In these circumstances there are usually so many forces and drivers at work, and so many powerful stakeholders involved, that the sum of all their interaction is impossible to model satisfactorily. In these situations it is more helpful to use 'soft' or qualitative futures. These draw directly on the experience and judgement of people who are involved in the system we want to understand. One of the most powerful soft futures processes is the kind of behavioural or 'open simulations' that Loop2 uses.

Open simulations are based on the premise that what happens in complex social systems is the product of formal and informal negotiation and bargaining between large numbers of stakeholders representing national, professional, institutional and personal interests. To replicate this negotiating process two key ingredients are needed: a set of participants representative of those in the real world; and a fictional but realistic operating environment for them to work in. There is no 'role play' – having to imagine how someone might think or react; participants are asked to take a position in the simulation that mirrors their own so that their behaviour is accurately informed by their 'real-life' insights and experience. As in real life, open simulations allow conventions, structures and rules to be challenged and renegotiated, and the only rules that apply are those that already govern the players in their everyday work, such as legal obligations or the regulations relating to organisational or professional conduct.

Open simulations are like a giant version of the flight simulators used to train pilots: they offer a highly realistic but safe learning environment for the 'crew' that is flying it (in our case, approximately 70 players). What happens in the simulation is less important than the insights and learning that participants and moderators generate together after the experience. It provides one of the most robust ways of understanding how complex social systems respond to large-scale and rapid change and was therefore the perfect tool for helping to understand how the NHS might respond to the reform agenda.

The Windmill simulation design

The Windmill 2007 simulation explored two time periods. The first round covered the financial year 2008/9. This involved making some assumptions about how the health care system might have developed by that time. The second round covered 2010/11. The year's gap gave the design team the opportunity to refocus the play with the 'rules' and issues drawn from the first round.

The design team recognised that, even with the considerable weight of policy guidance on health system reform, there are still some areas where the 'rules' by which health care is planned, commissioned, delivered and regulated are either ill defined or are capable of being interpreted in different ways. However, to ensure that we used realistic assumptions for the first round, and that the Windmill participants explored the relevant issues, we held some initial discussions with leading policy-makers, clinicians and regulators. Their views proved invaluable in focusing attention on the significant questions about the future direction of the English health system.

The Windmill 'patch'

The Windmill 2007 simulation was set in a hypothetical but realistic context that had been specifically designed for the event. The mythical county of Glicestershire is located in the Central Strategic Health Authority (SHA). Windmill 2007 focused on two of the primary care trusts (PCTs) in the Central SHA: the larger Glicestershire County PCT, and Ellerton PCT, which shared its boundaries with the unitary authority, Ellerton City Council. The PCTs had differing starting points, with Glicestershire PCT already working with its provider services at 'arm's length' and with active groups of practices involved in practice-based commissioning. Ellerton PCT, by contrast, was more actively involved with its in-house services, and PCT locality managers tended to lead practice-based commissioning.

The area included health care provision offered by three NHS trusts: Glicestershire Hospitals NHS Foundation Trust, St Gerald's University Hospitals NHS Trust, and Stellar Healthcare NHS Trust. A range of independent sector providers was also included: an independent sector treatment centre; a conventional private provider that also provided mobile diagnostics and surgery; and a provider of GP out-of-hours services. The data supporting the descriptions of the organisations was drawn from actual NHS organisations but the names were changed to encourage participants to think laterally rather than be constrained by any knowledge of that health system.

In light of the issues that our advisory group (the participants of the first workshop) wanted the Windmill project to explore, the simulation was set up in terms of structure and players to allow the market to run (more or less well) on the current policy trajectory. We did not build in the possibility of a complete policy reversal with a return to a centrally planned and managed service.

The Windmill contributors

To make the simulation manageable the 'real world' was simplified by reducing the number of organisations and players that would typically exist in it and by narrowing the range of issues being tackled. This meant that some aspects of health care were represented by fewer players than in real life: this was particularly true of the clinical input, political stakeholders and the full range of public and patient interests. The participants – managers, clinicians and policy-makers – were drawn from organisations across England. They were chosen because of their prior interest in how the health care system would evolve rather than for any particular perspective on what should happen.

Part 2: The Windmill messages for the future health care system

In this section of the report we focus on the main learning points drawn from the various stages of the Windmill process, and from the discussions with the Windmill participants during and after the simulation, as well as from the views and observations of a wider range of commentators in the meetings that followed. All of the contributors' suggestions have helped us to move from 'what happened' to 'what should happen next' in order that the latest round of health reforms can deliver sustainable organisational and financial performance and real benefits for patients. The series of meetings and the learning drawn from the simulation experience has focused our thinking on nine key issues.

- **Free trade or protectionism?** The health system reforms have introduced market principles and processes into what essentially has been a state-run monopoly for more than 50 years. It has taken a huge investment but we are now arguably at the 'tipping point' where a regulated market could deliver improvements for patients. However, some managers and clinicians behave as if they want to revert to central control and provider protectionism. Forcing the system to cope with two incompatible sets of rules and incentives would court disaster. This ambiguity needs to be resolved if the reforms are to deliver their intended benefits.

- **A regulated and managed market in the interests of patients** All legal markets are regulated to some extent to promote competition and to protect the interests of consumers. The health care system is no exception but, as the market evolves with the spread of foundation trusts, the respective roles of Monitor, the Healthcare Commission and the SHAs need to be clarified and given greater focus to ensure that competition and contestability work in the public interest and that patients' interests are paramount.

- **PCTs are not currently set up for effective commissioning** While health care providers seem increasingly prepared to respond to market-based incentives, commissioners appear to be analytically underpowered and nervous about destabilising existing provider networks. They are not yet able to be 'impartial commissioners' on behalf of their populations.

- **The role of the independent sector** The independent sector was encouraged into the NHS because it would help establish conditions of contestability and had the potential to bring innovation, expertise and responsiveness into the system. However, the willingness of these new entrants to endure extended, costly and indecisive procurement processes cannot be taken for granted. Private providers need to appreciate some of the constraints to decision-making within PCTs; however, commissioners equally need to understand the way in which businesses think about procurement and its costs. Without this mutual understanding there is a risk that private providers will stop working with the NHS, taking with them their flexible capacity and removing a powerful competitive driver from the system.

- **Social enterprise – a missed opportunity?** The government has supported the development of social enterprise as a means of combining commercial rigour with the benefits and values of the third sector. However, within the NHS, the model is poorly understood – by both commissioners and providers – and it is questionable whether social enterprise will operate on a scale that will enable it to become the model for mainstream service providers.

- **Improving the quality of primary care** There are early signs that the GP contract and the Quality and Outcomes Framework (QOF) scheme have brought improvements to the quality of primary care. However, they are unlikely to be effective at tackling poor performance and, on their own, they will not do enough to develop services. Greater use of contracting through Personal Medical Services (PMS), Alternative PMS (APMS) and Specialist Provider Medical Services (SPMS) arrangements could help to deliver improvements in accessibility, skill mix and a wider range of locally based services.

- **Size matters for primary care commissioning and provision** Practice-based commissioning has the potential to encourage a wider range of health care to be delivered outside hospitals. However, the current model of small independent practices operating on their own or in a jointly owned company or co-operative does not offer a consistent or sustainable basis for significant shifts in the way health care is delivered. Significant scaling-up and strengthening of primary care organisation is needed for both commissioning and service delivery. The key question is whether primary care practices will be able to achieve this aggregation on their own or whether other partners or alternative sources of investment are needed.

- **Public and patient engagement** The approach to patient and public engagement needs to take advantage of, and reflect, the increased reliance on market forces. A step change is needed in commissioners' understanding of public and patient views. Commissioners and providers need to survey patient experiences and feed this back into the design of their services. Commissioners should also consult on their commissioning intentions and local priorities. However, the current formal arrangements for reconfiguring services are clumsy and slow, and need to be reformed. As part of this, the government could consider removing the requirement for providers to consult formally on changes of service.

- **Improving public health** PCTs need to concentrate their health improvement efforts at reorienting the way in which health services protect and promote the health needs of their populations, and prevent illness, through commissioning. Action to address wider determinants of health and well-being would be better led by local authorities with support from PCTs and other partners, where appropriate. Interventions to address health and well-being should be subject to the same disciplines of commissioning as health care. Both aspects need strong support from public health professionals, but differentiating these tasks will help to ensure that health improvement is given a higher priority in public services.

We will now discuss these issues in more detail.

Free trade or protectionism?
The issues

■ The health system reforms have introduced market principles and processes into what essentially has been a state-run monopoly for 50 years. Perhaps it is not surprising that just as market forces begin to modernise service provision, the clamour (especially from institutional and professional interests) to stick with the status quo is reaching a climax. As with 19th-century Corn Law reform we have seen opinions in the system polarise into two camps: the 'free traders', who believe that choice, contestability and competition will provide the necessary impetus to modernise the system for the benefit of patients; and the 'protectionists', who want to regain control of the system in order to plan and manage it more directly.

■ Despite the government's efforts to introduce a market system into the health sector, it has taken time for managers and professionals to make the shift from a 'managed' to a 'market' culture. There are two reasons for this. The first is cultural: the strength of the public service ethos that attracted many managers and professionals to work in the NHS should not be under-estimated. It underpins ambiguous and sometimes sceptical reactions to the role that the private and third sector could play in delivering health care. Historically the health care system has demonstrated tendencies toward homoeostasis, and this set of reforms is no exception.

- The second reason concerns the way that the health system reforms are communicated. National health policy seems to be furthering the conflicting philosophies of 'free trade' and 'protectionism' at the same time. It is no accident that successive Secretaries of State have used different terminology to soften the impact of health system reform. The use of 'contestability' for 'competition' or 'system' for 'market' conveys messages that there is not wholesale enthusiasm for a regulated competitive market in health service provision. Whereas collaboration is seen as positive and to be encouraged, the centre is much less open about wanting to see a fair and competitive market in general and is unclear about the circumstances in which competition is in the patients' interests. Commissioners feel caught between being encouraged to innovate and demonstrate world-class commissioning on the one hand and being held responsible for the stability of local health care provision on the other. Many feel there are few rewards or incentives for those who 'rock the boat'.

- The current health system reforms were developed because of the failure of past attempts. These more centrally driven approaches to engineering change had serious limitations and showed signs of diminishing returns. Neither enhanced performance targets, nor strong investment in modernisation processes, nor massive increases in funding proved sufficient to deliver the transformation the government wanted to see in the NHS. The service remained largely unresponsive to the needs and preferences of patients, with a limited ability to respond to rising consumer expectations and to secure innovation and productivity from providers.

- Considerable time and resources have now been invested in designing and building a managed health care market. There are

signs that managers and professionals are becoming more supportive of the new change levers at their disposal and, although it is still early days, there is some evidence that patients are beginning to see the benefits that greater choice and plurality of supply can offer.

What needs to be done?

■ It is too soon to pronounce publicly on the degree to which the use of market forces has been a success or otherwise. Nor is it the time to give mixed messages – ambiguity brings the worst of both worlds: the costs of competitive processes without any of the benefits that could be delivered. If the government wishes to see a health care market that is managed and regulated in the interests of patients, it needs to give a clear, unambiguous commitment to this. This commitment needs to come from the top: both from the Secretary of State for Health and from the Chief Executive of the NHS.

A regulated and managed market in the interests of patients

The issues

■ All legal markets are regulated to some extent to promote competition, deal with market failure and protect the interests of consumers. In the retail sector, for example, the Office of Fair Trading (OFT) keeps a close watch on the largest supermarket chains to ensure that they do not monopolise the market adversely, thereby threatening consumer interests and choice. A market for health services is no exception and requires effective regulation to prevent potential abuse of monopoly powers and supplier caballing.

■ Markets in services that are emerging from monopoly state provision require particularly sensitive regulation, and protecting the public interest is critical in health care. However, whereas regulation in other sectors is focused on ensuring that adequate levels of competition are maintained to protect consumers, in the NHS there is a sense that market regulation is intended to limit the effects of competition.

- Our commentators suggested that the problem relates to a lack of clarity about the differences between market regulation and market management, and that this confusion is suffused throughout the health service. When we pushed them for workable definitions, market regulation appeared relatively well understood. It is a function that oversees the workings of the market to protect the public interest and, critically, is usually performed by a body on the authority of (but independent from) government. This body has to be 'above' the market; it ought not to be enmeshed in the exchanges between purchasers, providers and consumers, but should be able to arbitrate between them.

- Market management, by contrast, is seen as the process by which purchasers – if they are able to exert some control over the market – ensure that there are sufficient providers to produce genuine competition for their contracts and that 'provider capture' is avoided. The purchasers will also manage the market by deciding when to stimulate new market entry and when to support an existing provider to enable them to develop new services, or simply to maintain supply.

- Using this definition PCTs should logically undertake the market management role in the NHS as they make the commissioning/purchasing decisions and understand the dynamics of the local health economy. However, whether or not they have the ability, capacity and breadth of view to do this in an evidence-based, risk-bearing way is debatable.

- The SHAs' behaviour in relation to market management is very important if the current structure of commissioning is to be maintained. If, as we suggest, PCTs are responsible for market management, the SHAs undoubtedly have a performance management role to ensure that PCTs exercise this properly. Our commentators were concerned that the SHAs' performance management role might extend to taking over the market management role themselves, which would shift the purchasing decisions out of the local setting. Although this might have advantages of costs, scale and influence, it would raise key questions about the role of, and the need for, the PCT layer in the system.

- There were concerns, both in the simulation and in the subsequent discussions, that whoever manages the market has to ensure there is a demonstrably fair and competitive environment for all providers. If the private sector is going to be excluded from a market in favour of NHS or foundation trust providers, commissioners should do so in a way that makes the exclusion public from the start, as well as justifying the reasons for not considering private sector offers. The private sector considered this approach to be preferable to 'informal exclusions', which often mean that financial risks cannot be properly assessed, and considerable bidding costs are raised without any real prospect of recovery.

- With regard to the market regulation function in health care there are three candidates: the Healthcare Commission, Monitor and the SHAs. The Healthcare Commission satisfies our regulator requirements in that it assesses performance of providers and commissioners across the whole health care system. Importantly, its regulatory functions are applied irrespective of the ownership of the provider (NHS, foundation trust, private and third sectors) or of the source of the funding (self-pay, private medical insurance and through the NHS). The precise role of 'OfCare' – the anticipated successor to the Healthcare Commission – is as yet unclear but, it has been suggested that it could act as the economic regulator. However, its role as independent assessor of the health system's performance (no matter how that system is designed) would be compromised if it were at the same time engaged in regulating market entry, handling market failure, setting tariffs and the like.

■ The original role of Monitor was to ensure that NHS trusts that were granted the autonomy of foundation status were economically and managerially 'fit for purpose'. In the simulation, Monitor was cast as 'bondholder': that is, it was principally interested in making sure that the state received an appropriate return on its assets. However, as the simulated time passed, Monitor began to act (often at the behest of others as the financial situation tightened) more like a 'shareholder' with greater interest in the governance of foundation trusts as well as influencing the shape of the provider market through mergers and acquisitions. The next progression might have been for it to take on the role of the 'holding company' with a much more direct interest in the management of its 'subsidiaries'. This move to management by Monitor was considered a step too far, however, because it would become in effect a monopoly provider in the market rather than a regulator of it.

■ In the discussions it was clear that, because of Monitor's responsibilities in relation to assessments and compliance, it was pursuing its objectives in its stewardship role by taking this more 'engaged' stance. Foundation trusts – even the best – were seen to be at the beginning of a journey in learning to be business-like about the delivery of health care. If Monitor were to revert to a disinterested bondholder and not continue to develop the economic and business capabilities of foundation trusts, there was a fear that many would fail and would revert to some form of state control. Not having the full range of autonomous providers would mean that the state's ability to use any form of contestability to drive economies in the health service would be severely hampered.

- As it is currently structured, Monitor can oversee only its section of the provider side of the market and therefore cannot act as economic regulator of the whole health system. However, given that in the future foundation trusts will provide such a large proportion of acute services – and increasingly mental health and community care services – the significance of Monitor's transitional role in ensuring that the foundation trust providers are competent cannot be over-estimated. Its work will be crucial to the success of the reforms and the effective working of the market; in its current form, it is not designed to be the economic regulator of the whole system, although given its independence it might be developed to perform this function in the future.

- In the simulation many players expected the SHAs to take on the market regulation role. In the discussions that followed it was felt that the ability of the SHAs to act as a market regulator is compromised on two counts: they are directly overseen by the centre; and, because they performance manage commissioning by PCTs, they are themselves players in the market. It was also felt unlikely that SHAs would be able to act independently of government, especially if they had to choose between protecting an existing provider pattern (and the stability that went with it) and allowing competition to disturb that pattern, with the consequential risk of 'political noise'.

- Beyond these three immediate candidates for market regulation there are two other players that we could not incorporate into the Windmill simulation but which featured in most of the conversations afterwards: the OFT and the European Union (EU). There was much discussion about the legal status of foundation trusts, about whether NHS commissioning and procurement represented a legal definition of a market, and what stance the EU might take on state protection of state-owned providers. Although the OFT was seen as too blunt an instrument to be the sole economic regulator of the health market, it was thought to be only a matter of time before the provision of health services to the NHS would fall within the remit of these more general European regulatory regimes.

■ In all the conversations after the event, the lack of clarity of the SHA role was raised. Ministers (and those who work for them) will undoubtedly expect their intermediate tier to have a comprehensive understanding of the local workings of the system – largely through the commissioning side. But given the weakness of the commissioning function, they are not currently positioned or equipped to take on this role in the future. In the simulation the SHA players said they felt frustrated because they did not have oversight of the whole system, partly because the PCTs resented their interference and partly because, as more providers became foundation trusts, they naturally became progressively 'blinder' to the provider side of the system. Without strengthening their relationships on the commissioning side of the system, SHAs will not be able to conduct this oversight function or what was described as 'tone-setting leadership'.

■ There was a concern that the SHAs might react to the 'blindness' by strengthening their hold over the foundation trusts by interpreting 'market oversight' as 'market management' and 'market management' as 'performance management' of the foundation trusts. This shift from oversight to management would mean that the state once again controlled both the demand and supply sides of the health system, that any chance of using commissioning, contestability and patient choice to drive up efficiency and increase responsiveness to consumers would be lost and we would be back where we started in 1997.

What needs to be done?

- The field of market regulation is both crowded and uncertain. There needs to be clarity about the longer-term roles of and relationships between the SHAs, the Healthcare Commission's successor 'OfCare' and Monitor. These will be determined in part by the degree to which governments believe that the considerable investment already made in the introduction of market-like incentives into the NHS will go on to deliver improved productivity and greater sensitivity to consumers. Monitor currently has two levers of influence – governance mechanisms (which holds boards to account) and the manipulation of market incentives. Although the former may be relatively effective as NHS trusts move into foundation status, over time an independent economic regulator will have to rely more on incentives such as competition rules and the tariff.

- The Department of Health (DH) – as a matter of some urgency – has to provide a clear set of rules for competition in health care to ensure that the system works in the interests of patients and so that everybody – purchaser and provider, public and private – is able to plan for the future. Without that the system will stall – unable to judge risks and benefits and therefore unable to develop strategies for investment and disinvestment. These rules – and a clear explanation of them – are also important to citizens so that they can judge how well their health system is performing.

- As part of that clarification of the rules, if it is indeed inevitable that the NHS will enter the domain of mainstream economic regulation as has been suggested, the implications and consequences of a more direct role for the OFT, and more particularly for the EU, need to be understood, accepted and planned for.

- Again as part of the clarification of the rules, the 'public benefit' nature of foundation trusts needs to be addressed. In the simulation, as foundation trusts become more successful they may accumulate financial reserves. There has to be a well-understood process for an economic regulator to determine whether management is using all the assets of the organisation – including cash reserves – for the public good.

- The handling of market failure has been the subject of a great deal of discussion by policy-makers but it remains unclear how struggling provider trusts will be handled. If a foundation trust is involved it is assumed that this is a role for Monitor, but there do not appear to be any clear principles for handling mergers and acquisitions, nor is there clarity about the type of organisations that would be considered suitable for taking on the management of a failing NHS trust or a foundation trust. Market failure is not only a governance and financial problem, it is potentially a threat to the continued supply of services to patients. PCTs need to be actively involved in maintaining access.

- Irrespective of how the role of economic regulation is performed, there are some important issues that the Healthcare Commission (or OfCare) will need to have considered in its assessment of the performance of the system. First, it needs to extend its work to cover the regulation of primary care provider services if patients are to have confidence in the quality of services delivered outside hospital. Second, it needs to ensure there is a process for the rapid licensing of providers wishing to enter the health care market without a track record of performance, and also to re-register existing providers where new supply chain alliances or new governance arrangements have been formed.

- An important question for them is whether the assessment of health care performance can be adequately undertaken solely with an organisational focus. Increasingly, patients will be cared for by competing 'supply chains' of providers, and it may be necessary for regulators to take a more 'horizontal' service view rather than a vertical institutional perspective in order to assess safety and quality.

- If PCTs are to adopt the role of market manager within the government's competition rules discussed above, then the implications for the development of the SHA role are considerable. The SHAs will need to work with PCTs in:
  - ensuring local health systems protect and promote patient and citizen interests
  - determining the level of competition needed to drive up economies and enhance patient services
  - incentivising new players to contribute to better care locally
  - assessing the risks and opportunities of market exits and entries
  - evaluating the comparative performance of its commissioners in delivering improved productivity and health outcomes.

In doing this, SHAs will have to be careful not to 'emasculate' PCTs in the eyes of the other stakeholders. SHAs may need to negotiate acceptable ways of working with each PCT according to local circumstances so that points of intervention and flows of information to and from the SHA run smoothly and serve to enhance not diminish the authority of PCTs.

The financial regime

The issues

- While a tariff system offers a stable basis for the operation of the health care market, it does not provide a sound basis for negotiating between commissioners and providers. The tariff might be challenged from two directions: providers needing to address their costs may start to define more closely what is or is not included within the tariff price; and those who are more interested in attracting a higher volume of work may try to bundle in additional benefits that are appealing to patients and GPs.

- Tariffs could offer the centre a direct lever to stimulate health care productivity. Indeed, the purpose of a tariff system is to offer an incentive to providers to increase their operating surplus in the short term by reducing costs, although in the longer term this will reduce the tariff. However, the lever needs to be used sensitively. Since tariffs are based on average costs, sudden, centrally imposed drops in tariff may have significant consequences, even for those who are operating just below tariff prices. Such reductions may trigger withdrawal from services and reduce the flexibility that local commissioners require. There is a prior order question, however, as to who sets the tariff. If a national independent regulator of the whole health economy existed, then it may be that tariff-setting might be more appropriately undertaken by them (as in other regulated industries) than by either the Department of Health or the SHAs.

- In the simulation there were two market mechanisms at work. The first was patient choice with money following patients, which proved to be an extremely powerful stimulator of change. The second was PCTs commissioning large-scale, long-term contracts from a range of providers. It was interesting that the apparent incompatibility of the two mechanisms was overlooked. The two approaches led to very different dynamics in the system. On the one hand, under 'choice', licensed providers were trying to understand and satisfy the needs and preferences of individual consumers with minimal intervention from the PCT. On the other hand, 'contestability' meant that large commissioning bodies offered fairly long-term contracts to a competing pool of large-scale providers. There is clearly a limit to the range of services to which the 'choice' model can apply, but in the discussions after the simulation it was clear that for the PCTs and providers, competing for a market (contestability) was a much easier and less risky proposition than competing within a market (patient choice). Taking this 'easy' route, however, could mean that the interests of health care providers and commissioners would prevail over those of individual patients if it meant that they did not have a choice over how and where they were treated and by whom.

What needs to be done?

- More effective ways of introducing change in the financial regime may involve commissioners in small experiments in price negotiation for relatively standard procedures to test market sensitivity; but care must be taken to avoid compromising the integrity of the tariff in the rest of the system.

- In the long term it may be that tariffs are set by an independent economic regulator, but in the meantime the DH needs to exercise caution in the way in which it uses the tariff lever. There needs to be sound evidence, or at least modelling, about the impact that proposed changes would have on innovation and quality, and about the point at which the local system becomes unstable. If the tariffs are not to be set independently, then SHAs would be better placed to carry out this level of economic regulation as it is they who could undertake the detailed analysis of the local impact of any deliberate change in tariff levels.

- If there is to be a move away from patients exercising choice wherever feasible and towards commissioner-driven contestability, care will be needed to ensure that providers continue to worry about how to understand and satisfy the needs and preferences of individual patients and users. It may be that, no matter how competent and knowledgeable the commissioners become, it is the consumers themselves who will provide the most effective long-term engine for service improvement.

PCTs are not currently set up for effective commissioning

The latest round of reforms is heavily dependent on the existence of effective and impartial commissioning. The intended aims of commissioning are to maximise health gains for the population, minimise health inequalities, and ensure the efficient delivery of accessible, appropriate and responsive services that represent value for money. There are high expectations that the new PCTs will rise to the challenge and redefine the way in which commissioning is undertaken. There is a new set of change levers to support it, and the engagement of GP practices in practice-based commissioning is intended to provide a basis for clinical dialogue and challenge. Will the latest incarnation of commissioning deliver on expectations?

The issues

■ PCTs do not yet seem able to act as impartial commissioners on behalf of their populations. The evidence from the simulation and the other events suggests they are nervous about destabilising local services. Some have an ambivalence about the role of the independent sector and, because they have continuing responsibility for a large industry of in-house services, they may be less willing to exploit the benefits that encouraging a diverse range of providers with some competition and contestability could offer to patient care.

■ Where PCTs do have opportunities to commission new service models or bring in additional or alternative providers, there is a danger that protracted decision-making could jeopardise the continuing interest of the independent sector, which may no longer see the delivery of NHS services as a viable business.

■ PCTS appear to be reluctant to push for greater patient choice and allow money to follow patients in the way envisaged in government policy. Although the idea of choice as a driver for efficiencies is acknowledged, we have seen subtle changes in language, with the term 'contestability' being used in preference to the harder 'competition'. The implication is that, rather than having competition within a market, it is acceptable, or even easier, to restrict market forces to competition for a market.

■ While practice-based commissioning offers the opportunity to bring new thinking, clinical challenge and innovation to the commissioning process, in reality it is largely focused on the opportunities for marginal shifts of activity from secondary to primary care and on enhancing diagnostic services for GPs. PCTs have limited means for either stimulating and encouraging practice-based commissioning or managing its performance. The latter is crucial if some of the potential conflicts of interest between the commissioning and provider roles in primary care are to be limited.

■ The coterminosity between PCTs and local authorities provides a sound basis for joint commissioning. However, these commissioning processes still appear to be negotiated in parallel with practice-based commissioning. Work still needs to be carried out in thinking through how the different levels and types of commissioning will interact.

There are several reasons why we are not yet seeing evidence of impartial commissioning and responsive decision-making.

■ Health care providers have an increasingly sophisticated grasp of their activity, capacity and the costs of production. By contrast, PCTs lack the analytical and planning skills and are insufficiently resourced to offer an effective and consistent challenge as commissioners.

■ A second factor is the strong legacy of NHS culture. The deep-seated public service ethos that attracted many managers and professionals to work in the NHS sometimes leads to an ambivalent or sceptical view of the role that the private and third sector could play in delivering health care. Many senior managers still feel accountable for system stability and for limiting local political reaction to service changes. There is still a feeling that there are few rewards or incentives for those who 'rock the boat'.

- A lack of experience in handling negotiations and relationships with the independent sector is partly to blame for slow and protracted decision-making. Too often there is an adversarial approach to contracting, with a focus on tasks and money, but with limited interest in innovation, outcomes, ongoing relationships with suppliers or the important processes that need to be in place to make any new services work well. As one private provider commented: 'We would prefer a dance rather than a game of tennis.' NHS foundation trusts also complain that there is little understanding of how to maximise benefit from the commissioning–provider relationship.

- Building consensus across all stakeholders might be a valuable outcome, if it could be achieved, but not if it became an end in itself, further extending the decision-making process. It can sometimes seem that if PCTs can gain agreement from all parties about the 'right thing to do', they will protect themselves from any direct accountability for decisions, particularly those that may adversely affect particular service providers.

- It is also difficult for PCTs to be impartial commissioners when they have a dual role as service providers. While PCTs have been encouraged to put their provider services on an 'arm's length' basis, in reality this could be better described as 'finger's length'. Structural solutions and 'devolved budgets' are not a demonstration of a true commissioning relationship. Retaining provider services not only compromises commissioning impartiality, it also distracts PCT energy, which should be devoted to developing the commissioning function.

What needs to be done

- Commissioning will become more effective in the context of the market reforms only if PCTs have a clear, unambiguous commitment to and focus on their role as impartial purchasers on behalf of their population. If the market-based mechanisms and other reforms are to be given a fair trial, there needs to be much greater clarity about the commissioning role, and clear expectations from the DH and SHAs that PCTs and their practice-based commissioners will use the new levers of benchmarking, patient choice and competition for the benefit of their population.

- PCTs and providers need to recognise their separate roles and, importantly, respect each other's (regulated) autonomy. For PCTs this means relinquishing any vestigial responsibility for the fate of providers.

- PCTs need investment in organisational development and must have significantly strengthened analytical resources and skills if they are to perform their commissioning responsibilities effectively. They need to improve their performance very quickly. The independent sector has a valuable role to play in stimulating and developing commissioning. Those with a track record of commissioning in other contexts and in other countries bring useful analytical skills and techniques, rigour, and commercial acumen and capacity to help to fast track the development of NHS commissioning. There are three specific areas that need attention.

  - First, PCT managers and clinicians need to develop greater skills in 'business thinking'. This includes a greater appreciation of how NHS providers and the independent sector work, and their key motivations. PCTs also need to develop their negotiating skills to include concerns about relationships as well as tasks.

  - Second, PCTs need to rethink what their planning function is for. They need to shift from a service planning approach, with its focus on what gets done on which hospital site or in what type of community facility, to concentrate on planning for commissioning. This involves modelling needs and demands, understanding patient expectations and preferences, considering technical and clinical innovation, and looking at what outcomes are desirable. Service planning, together with analysis of market and financial risks, is a provider-side activity.

- Third, PCTs need to develop robust processes and measures for monitoring practice-based commissioning and for stimulating its effectiveness. There needs to be clarity about the full range of commissioning activities that commissioning clusters undertake, to avoid a narrow focus on those that offer the greatest benefits to primary care. For those commissioning clusters that are active and ambitious, a willingness to discuss the next stage of their evolution will help to maintain their interest and commitment. Models where commissioning groups are allocated full-population funding may well offer a good mix of incentives for preventive health care, but they also generate significant risks to the NHS, and therefore need further debate.

The role of the independent sector
The issues

Most NHS providers are ready and willing to face competition and are becoming more 'business focused' in the way in which they are thinking about the future. However, they face a number of constraints in their ability to respond effectively in a market context. By contrast, at least some independent sector providers are becoming increasingly concerned about whether providing services to the NHS is worth their while.

- Both NHS and independent providers share a common concern (albeit from a different perspective) that there is not a fair competitive environment for health care provision funded by the NHS.

- There are concerns that there is differential treatment of the NHS and private sector in terms of the Healthcare Commission's standards' requirements and associated inspection regime.

- For NHS providers a key constraint on their ability to respond quickly to shifts in the health care market – such as changes produced by patients exercising choice – is the requirement to undertake lengthy, formal public consultations.

- For the independent sector the perception is that NHS commissioners either do not trust private sector providers or are resistant to their role in delivering mainstream care to NHS patients. As highlighted above this may reflect PCT concerns about provider failure and the vestigial sense of responsibility that commissioners feel for local NHS providers. However, the net effect is that some independent operators feel that they are deliberately kept as marginal players or are used only to overcome short-term performance problems.

- By contrast with commissioners, NHS providers appear more willing to work with and forge partnerships with their independent sector colleagues.

- There is a danger that independent providers will withdraw from the NHS market, taking with them their capacity, innovation and ability to respond quickly to changes in demand and need. A further danger is that potential new entrants will be discouraged from investing in this area.

What needs to be done

- NHS commissioners need to develop greater awareness of the impact that their decision-making will have on the willingness of independent sector and not-for-profit providers to stay with the NHS market. One potential sticking point is how they are treated within the patient choice system. When it comes into effect in 2008, the policy that offers patients a free choice of NHS or approved independent sector provider will deliver its true objectives only if the way in which patients are offered choices moves away from the limited 'front-page' menu system.

■ As commissioners become more sensitive to the time and cost impact on independent providers of extended negotiation and decision timetables, independent providers need to accept the multiple and often conflicting objectives of the NHS, its need to ensure local access to services and the highly charged political context in which it operates.

■ Independent providers need to recognise the importance of developing local relationships in furthering their health care business. In the future it is unlikely that there will be large central procurements for services. The opportunities for business development are through the PCT commissioning route, but they may also arise through practice-based commissioners, partnerships with foundation trusts or joint ventures with social enterprises and third sector organisations.

■ If there are ongoing fears about the private sector 'cherry picking' the most profitable aspects of NHS care, this can be addressed relatively simply by reforming pricing mechanisms. The Payment by Results fixed tariff system could be refined in some areas to move away from average NHS costs to a normative 'cost-effective' price that reflects good clinical practice and an assessment of achievable unit costs.

■ NHS health care providers need to continue to develop the 'business-thinking' skills of lead doctors and directorate managers. Ensuring that they understand their costs, production processes and income for each service line will mean they will be well prepared to respond to shifts in demand or tariff changes. Linked to this, NHS providers need to gain a better understanding of what constitutes their core business, differentiating what they have to do themselves from those areas where other parties or partners could help to deliver elements of patient care more efficiently.

Social enterprise – a missed opportunity?

The issues

- Social enterprise, as a relatively new form of organising the delivery of public services for public benefit, has been high on the government's agenda for some time. The attraction is the potential for this organisational form to combine the benefits of commercial rigour with the social benefits and values of the third sector.

- A key difficulty for social enterprise is that the model is still poorly understood within the NHS, not least by commissioners. There is confusion about governance and management, the legal models involved, the role of profit in social enterprises and the 'public benefit' aspect of their status. If they have been 'spun out' of PCTs there are also concerns about there being sufficient independence from the 'host' organisation – in both financial and governance terms – for them to operate in a market.

- Impartial commissioners may be unwilling to contract with social enterprise providers if there are concerns about the small scale of the services they offer and about how robust or stable the organisations might be in the longer term. Also raised was the issue of regulation – if social enterprise organisations are independent of PCTs, then what is the appropriate regulatory and accountability regime for them?

- Social enterprises that are formed to take on PCT provider services face particular challenges. There are tensions between being small and locally focused and the desire to become larger, more stable organisations that might have a greater impact. There may be restrictions on their ability to borrow and these will present some limits to their ability to grow, and partnering has to be carefully approached if the whole philosophy of the enterprise is not be compromised. This makes it all the more important that social enterprises are properly designed and established in the first instance. Simply transferring services with an outdated service model or ongoing performance problems into a social enterprise is unlikely to be successful.

■ There are also risks that clinicians and managers who transfer to social enterprises may be enthusiastic about the idea of greater freedom to act, but may lack the business competence and confidence to ensure the enterprise thrives and is sustainable in the longer term.

What needs to be done

■ Health care professionals involved in the establishment of social enterprise need to consider carefully what assets and resources are transferred from existing services to avoid these becoming liabilities. They also need to ensure they are not protected by a 'golden contract' from their previous employers that, once withdrawn, exposes them to a great deal of risk. Similarly, if enterprises are set up as co-owned with staff, it is important that everybody understands the difference between management and ownership.

■ As employers, PCTs have a duty to prepare their directly employed staff to work at arm's length or outside the NHS. In addition the Royal Colleges and other bodies that represent and lead the professions might consider making a shift from campaigning against the current set of reforms to enabling their members to understand and prepare for them. As the leaders of the professions they might consider supporting their members in developing the necessary business skills to enable them to work effectively in the new health care environment, whether in social enterprises or in mainstream NHS services. If they do not help their members to make an effective contribution to the management and development of services in the new environment, the professionals and the professional bodies themselves risk losing influence.

■ While there is scope to improve awareness among commissioners about the role that social enterprises can play in service delivery, social enterprises themselves need to focus their negotiations on the specific service delivery benefits and outcomes they are offering rather than the assumed benefits that their governance and value system bring.

Improving the quality of primary care
The issues

■ Primary care providers are scripted to play an increasingly important role in providing health care and diagnostic services beyond large acute hospitals. At the same time there is a strong impetus for the greater devolution of commissioning to GP practices, prompted by a desire to align spending decisions with budgetary responsibility. However, this combination of commissioning and providing roles is not without its risks.

■ While some active practices are seizing the opportunities presented by commissioning and the potential for extending their provider services, there are many others that are content with the benefits they gain from the new contract and see little incentive for their involvement in commissioning for their patients.

■ For those practices that use their commissioning powers to expand the range and volume of services they deliver (either as individual practices or as a collaborative group), there is the potential to improve the accessibility and perhaps the quality of care for their patients. However, there are several areas of concern.

– Health care services provided by GP practices are not subject to the same licensing and inspection regimes as independent or NHS-provided services. This makes it difficult for patients to access information about their comparative quality.

- There are also risks that GPs as commissioners and providers of services may have conflicts of interest in advising patients on their choices, and such conflicts are difficult to detect and regulate.

- This conflict of interest could lead to a reduction in the level of patient trust in their GP.

■ While there have been some improvements in access and appointment arrangements in primary care as a result of government and contractual initiatives, there is still a long way to go to meet public preference for extended opening hours and a wider range of services. Currently the levers for improved performance are the contract itself and the potential for patients to transfer between practices. Neither has so far proved very effective.

■ There is scope for PCTs to tender services through PMS, APMS and SPMS contracts, which could be used not only in under-doctored areas but also to establish new practices as competitors in areas of poor performance or limited access. However, there are two barriers.

- The first is the risks to PCTs of the impact that increasing contestability in primary care might have on their fledgling practice-based commissioning groups. With most practice-based commissioning groups in a very early stage of development, there are fears that opening up the provider side of primary care to new players could destabilise the commissioning relationships.

- The second is the requirement under existing contractual arrangements for PCTs to continue to pay for an element of practice costs even where lists have fallen as a result of patients exercising their right to transfer.

What needs to be done

THE COMMISSIONING ROLE

■ If practice-based commissioning focuses only on those areas of health care that can potentially be shifted from a hospital to a primary care setting, it will miss the opportunity to influence where the largest areas of health care resources are deployed. To be effective, practice-based commissioning needs to focus on the whole commissioning task.

■ If primary care is to rise to the challenge of more radical redesign of the service, and take on more extensive commissioning responsibilities (and budgetary accountability to match), it will need external support in commissioning expertise, systems, processes and, potentially, actuarial skills in understanding health risks and expenditure. This could come from PCTs if they can develop fast enough from commercial firms with commissioning skills.

THE PROVIDER ROLE

■ There are signs that improved responsiveness to patient needs and expectations of general practice can be achieved through opening up competition for patients between practices. This is an important lever for change that PCTs need to exploit more fully. While there are ways in which they can do this within the current rules, it would be easier to achieve if the requirements around guaranteed overhead payments to practices were removed and the entry of new providers to the primary care system made simpler. Given that the cost of market entry to general practice is relatively low, this could allow a revolution in the way in which primary care is delivered.

■ The current model of relatively small independent practices does not offer a sustainable base for a significant shift in the way health care is delivered. Nor do the collaborative organisations that many are forming to help them to undertake commissioning or provision offer a viable solution. The scaling-up of primary care through integration of primary care practices, PCT provider services and, potentially, NHS Local Improvement Finance Trust (LIFT) partners into a single organisation could offer the basis for tackling different standards in the quality of care. Such scaling-up could also be a means of integrating primary and community health services. A new legal entity would be needed to handle this, such as a community foundation trust, a community venture, or a limited company.

■ A call for 'scaling-up' in organisational terms, however, should not be interpreted as a requirement for centralising primary care into ever-larger premises. While health centres and polyclinics have an important role in allowing a wider range of care to be offered outside hospitals, for many patients, particularly older people, there will continue to be a need for local access to primary care, whether in traditional practices, supermarkets, mobile facilities or other public service outlets.

■ Alliances between primary medical services and other players offer some exciting possibilities that could accelerate the pace of change and improvement in primary care services for patients. With much of the success of the reforms hinging on practice-based commissioning and delivery of services closer to home, PCTs should give further consideration to ways of supporting and encouraging these alliances locally. One of the key questions is whether primary care practices are willing or able to undertake this themselves or whether an external catalyst is essential to delivering this level of change.

THE PERFORMANCE MANAGEMENT ROLE
■ As they support or stimulate more productive working models of primary care delivery, PCTs must also develop stronger processes for improving primary care provision and primary-care-led commissioning.

- PCTs also need to use all levers, sanctions and incentives that are currently available, including the option of stimulating greater contestability for primary care provision, in order to improve the quality and responsiveness of services to patients. Primary care might move to become a commissioned service in the same way as the delivery of acute or mental health services.

Public and patient engagement
The issues

- Although patient and public engagement structures have been repeatedly reorganised over the past ten years, the basic policy remains the same: commissioners and providers alike should undertake formal consultation on planned changes to health services with public and patient groups as well as local authority overview and scrutiny committees (OSCs). This policy fitted well into a system that was dominated by central target setting and planning. However, in the more dynamic environment of market mechanisms, patient choice and a regulatory framework, this requirement feels increasingly anachronistic.

- Patients find it difficult to understand the differences between commissioning and provision. Providers and commissioners have different interests and might conceivably be required to consult the public about contradictory proposals. For providers that need to introduce service changes in response to market shifts as a result of patient choice, the requirement to consult significantly affects their ability to respond quickly to changes in demand and puts them at a disadvantage compared with private sector competitors. How should an NHS provider respond to public opposition to changes that have been triggered by changes in patient choice?

- Members and governors in foundation trusts are drawn from staff, patients and the public; however, it is too early to draw conclusions about how effective these trusts will be. One idea that has been suggested is to require PCTs to establish a membership body along these lines. However, for organisations such as PCTs that establish health priorities, there is arguably a greater need to ensure that any such body is representative, a requirement that has bedevilled this area. Irrespective of how they are structured, these bodies struggle to achieve legitimacy and are always open to the charge that they represent no one but themselves. Whatever the merits of the foundation trust model, health and social care organisations can find it difficult to hear the authentic voice of the public through the formal representative bodies, and may well receive contradictory opinions that may or may not be informed by recent experience of health care.

■ One area that the public appears to be consistently concerned about, fuelled by media stories, is the existence of 'a postcode lottery'. The introduction of a more market-driven health system will inevitably exacerbate differences in what, how and where services are provided across the country. There is a delicate balance between the benefits that market forces can bring and the perceived loss of the 'N' in the NHS.

What needs to be done

■ PCTs as commissioners should be required to consult the public about their commissioning prospectus on, for example, a three-year cycle. The consultations need to stress the benefits that patients can expect to see, as well as the rationale for any exclusions.

■ The requirement to consult and account to local authority overview and scrutiny committees should be retained. OSCs should retain the right to be consulted about service changes and should continue to have a right to appeal to the Independent Reconfiguration Panel, although not necessarily to the Secretary of State for Health. OSCs may need to be strengthened with investment in leadership development and independent advice.

- The blanket requirements for NHS providers and commissioners to undertake lengthy statutory formal public consultation on service changes should be reviewed.

- Providers and commissioners should be expected to undertake market research on public opinion and patient satisfaction to ensure that the services they are developing are serving the needs and expectations of the public, including marginalised groups.

Improving public health
The issues

- The boundary changes to PCTs, ensuring that most are now coterminous with local authority partners, was intended to support greater focus on improving public health as well as integrating health and social care services. However, with significant pressure to deliver 'world-class commissioning' and a significant development agenda associated with this task, there are considerable risks that PCTs may give little time and energy to their health improvement responsibilities.

- Reducing health inequalities has been a government priority for some time, yet some conditions have shown a trend towards worsening performance. The Windmill process highlighted that, despite the rhetoric, commissioners find it difficult to ensure these objectives are at the heart of their commissioning processes.

- Our commentators felt that the time might have come to 'unbundle' the different facets of public health and the way in which these are led within public services. Historically many public health professionals have been more interested in health protection and health promotion than they have in improving the impact and effectiveness of health and social care services. However, the latter is an area where public health skills can make an essential contribution to commissioning.

- At practice-based commissioning level, giving the commissioning groups real funds for a real population could offer an effective incentive to improve health and therefore reduce demand on health services. Their interventions, however, are likely to be derived from a medical model rather than tackling wider factors that can influence inequalities in health status.

What needs to be done

- Health improvement and reducing health inequalities – the impact of both health and health care interventions – should be a stronger part of the performance management responsibilities of SHAs, working in partnership with government offices.

- PCTs and local authorities should be expected to extend their joint commissioning to health improvement interventions. Competition, contestability and formal commissioning have as much to offer the achievement of better health as they do the delivery of better health care.

- More work needs to be carried out to devise powerful incentives for commissioners to develop services that keep the population for which they are responsible as healthy as possible, as well as providing people with care and treatment when they are ill.

- Consideration should be given to separating responsibilities for different facets of health improvement. PCTs could retain their focus on health services, using their commissioning levers to ensure that health care is delivered in a way that promotes, protects and improves people's health and that reduces inequalities. The formal leadership of interventions that address the wider determinants of health and well-being could be assigned to local authorities.

Concluding observations

It will take time for managers and professionals to make the shift from a managed to a market culture. Providers appear better adjusted to the concept of competition and contestability, to benchmarking their services and responding to patient choice, at least in their outlook, if not yet always in delivery. Commissioners however, seem to be caught between the two systems: they are being encouraged to innovate and demonstrate 'world-class' commissioning, yet with expectations that their performance will be judged on the basis of managed system principles.

While politicians and policy-makers can naturally be impatient about how long things take to change, it is much too early to judge whether the experiment with market forces has failed. There may be those who would slow or reverse the reforms or, worse, allow mixed messages to be received. However, ambiguity brings the worst of both worlds – the costs of competitive processes without any of the benefits that could be delivered. The changes have yet to reach the 'tipping point'. Faltering now, so that two philosophies – a regulated market and a centrally managed system – are allowed to run at the same time is one of the greatest dangers facing the health care system in England. It could prove disastrous.

The limits of the market need to be spelled out, but its opportunities and benefits must also be emphasised, together with a commitment to bring in new providers and create a fair and equal environment in which they can operate. If the government wishes to see a health care market that is managed and regulated in the interests of patients, it needs to give a clear, unambiguous commitment to this. This commitment needs to come from the top: from both the Secretary of State for Health and the Chief Executive of the NHS.

Part 3: What happened in Windmill 2007 – how the teams reacted and what was learnt

The Windmill health system

The following organisations were represented in the Windmill health system:

- **The Department of Health (DH)** – in its revised streamlined form, working closely with colleagues in the SHA. One of the important issues that the DH was wrestling with was how to handle tariffs in the future

- **Monitor** – the foundation trust regulator. In the first round Monitor continued with its role in supporting the establishment of foundation trusts. In the second round, Monitor was given the role of NHS 'bondholder'

- **The Healthcare Commission** – working towards integration with the Commission for Social Care Inspection (CSCI), its challenge was how best to streamline health care regulation and continue to have an impact

- **Central Strategic Health Authority** – it had set its PCTs the challenge of demonstrating world-class commissioning. The SHA was also considering how it should behave as market manager

- **Glicestershire PCT** – a large and relatively high-performing PCT, recently established from two predecessor bodies

- **Glistening Primary Care Organisation (PCO)** – an ambitious, practice-based commissioning group keen to push the boundaries of responsibility for commissioning

- **Glicestershire Health Social Enterprise Unit** – recently established, this unit had taken on the provider services of

Glicestershire PCT. Unable to resolve issues around pension protection, the staff were technically on secondment

■ **Ellerton PCT** – sharing its boundaries with Ellerton Borough Council. Ellerton PCT was half-way through implementation of a tight recovery plan with its main acute provider, St Gerald's University Hospitals NHS Trust. It had retained its provider services, which were described as 'finger's length' rather than 'arm's length'

■ **Ellerton GPs and Locality Commissioning** – Ellerton PCT had strongly steered practice-based commissioning by establishing locality-based arrangements led by PCT managers

■ **Glicestershire Hospitals NHS Foundation Trust** – a two-site trust with reconfiguration plans that had yet to receive commissioner support. It had also lost activity to independent sector providers

■ **St Gerald's University Hospitals NHS Trust** – a large teaching hospital with a sprawling estate that needed consolidation. Its financial performance was poor but patients continued to rate the services highly

■ **Stellar Healthcare NHS Trust** – a high-performing trust with foundation trust aspirations, Stellar's main challenge was that it had a relatively small catchment for some services, which left it vulnerable to long-term sustainability. It had had some recent success in winning new business from local PCTs

■ **Patient Provident Private Hospital (PPP)** – part of a national private health care chain. PPP had recently diversified into wellness services and had taken over a leading provider of mobile diagnostic and theatre services

■ **Amalgam Health Plc** – an independent sector treatment centre (ISTC) provider with further interests as a provider of GP out-of-hours services

- **Unify Health International** – a provider of commissioning services that had also tested out the market for primary care provision

- **Chemico** – a national chain of chemists interested in expanding its traditional pharmacy role

- **Glicestershire and Ellerton Patients' Panel** – an active and assertive group of patient representatives

- **Glicestershire County Council** – a progressive council that was 'improving well', it was represented by the OSC and adult social services

- **The Glicestershire Gazette** – a local paper with a longstanding interest in local health stories.

Round one: 2008/9

Participants were given a detailed briefing on the Central SHA area, the health care organisations in the patch and their financial positions and performance, as well as the health challenges within the population. They were also ascribed a set of 'in-year' pressures to deal with in each of the two simulation rounds.

The context

The first round of the simulation started with a very similar context to that of 2007/8. National priorities were kept consistent, with the addition of two new developments.

- New capital rules were introduced that linked the amount of capital that trusts could access to their financial performance and operating surpluses.

- Patients had free choice of providers, and PCTs were being asked to support this actively.

Within the Central SHA area there were a number of pressures to which participants were asked to respond. These included the following.

- Health inequalities were highlighted as needing further attention, as did the continued demands placed on emergency care.

- Patient groups had raised serious concerns about the quality of older people's services in Glicestershire, presenting the foundation trust and social enterprise organisation with major change agendas.

- The quality of primary care in the city of Ellerton was highly variable and areas of poor performance needed to be tackled.

- PCTs were being encouraged to put their provider services on a more 'arm's length' basis.

- Centrally negotiated contracts with ISTCs were expiring, so any continued provision needed to be agreed with local PCTs.

In the remainder of this section we outline some of the developments that took place in the first simulation round.

Centre–local relations

- From the outset the DH took a 'pro-market' stance. This meant that it took a 'back-seat' position with little intervention as it was keen to see the market develop. Nevertheless, the DH found it difficult to resist introducing some early policy decisions to set a clear context for the 2008 round. Tariffs were reduced across the board and a new quality bonus introduced to offer commissioners a further lever in their negotiations with providers. Financial incentives for tackling health inequalities were also introduced. There was a clear message for health systems embarking on reconfiguration that there would be no ministerial intervention in what should be a local decision.

- At the end of 2008/9 the DH found that its role had become less interventionist. After a short period behaviours changed and it experienced less lobbying over policy changes than previously. The one exception was the level of tariff reduction: this managed to unite the SHA and Monitor, which were both concerned that the level of reduction could introduce too much system instability. They called for a more cautious and tailored approach to tariff reductions, backed by evidence of potential impact rather than blanket approaches to reduce costs and improve productivity.

- By contrast with the DH, the SHA took a more active role. Keen to set the right performance climate at an early stage, it issued PCTs and trusts with a specific set of performance objectives covering health outcomes, financial balance and restoring public confidence. By the year-end there were signs of progress on most of these. While the SHA felt well supported by the DH, which largely backed its approach, relationships locally and with the regulatory bodies proved more complex to negotiate. One of the key challenges was in establishing and maintaining an overview of what was happening across the Glicestershire health system. The SHA's perspective appeared to be assembled through its contacts with the PCTs as commissioners, yet even here it was challenged about whether its interventions were legitimate within the new market context or represented 'old-style' working. The provider side of the health system, with the mix of foundation trusts, social enterprise, primary care and independent sector companies, proved even more challenging territory for the SHA.

- Given this challenge, it was not surprising that, when faced with a range of proposals from PCTs and providers around different service strategies, the SHA attempted to resort to old-style planning. It did this by introducing a strategic review of 'the health picture of the future' that would provide a coherent vision of service changes across PCTs. The PCTs and providers largely resisted this as they felt it would lead to further delays in decision-making.

Health care regulation and market management

- The Healthcare Commission shifted its regulatory attention to commissioning, establishing a common registration and inspection platform for NHS and independent sector organisations, and a more targeted inspection regime that concentrated on organisations identified as high risks. This included trusts with significant financial difficulties.

- By the end of the year the Healthcare Commission found that independent sector organisations had demonstrated higher performance on core standards than the NHS. Their systematic approaches to delivering clinical care and commitment to achieving recognised standards put them ahead of their NHS rivals.

- A less positive finding was a review of the shift from secondary to primary care, which the Healthcare Commission concluded was stronger on intent than delivery. The review also found that inadequate investment in primary/community health premises was a significant constraint on the ability of PCTs and primary care providers to deliver the changes to which they were committed. However, the impact of this review appeared limited and it received little publicity or media coverage.

- In the same vein, Monitor also declared itself a light-touch regulator. To demonstrate this it relaxed the requirement on foundation trusts to consult with lead commissioning PCTs on any proposed changes to mandatory services, although Monitor stated that it would consider any objections to proposed changes on their own merits. Monitor's priorities focused on early discussions with potential foundation trusts, improving the financial capability of foundation trusts, and risk assessments, particularly for those organisations with private finance initiative (PFI) bids or that were seeking mergers and acquisitions.

- By the end of 2009 Monitor confirmed that its clear message to foundation trusts was to concentrate on having robust strategies for their core business. Monitor also recognised that it needed to pay far more attention to commissioning plans as a way of understanding risks to provider business, such as potential changes to market share. However, getting accurate information on which to make such judgements had proved challenging.

Commissioning a patient-led NHS?

- Both PCTs started off with clear intentions to deliver improved care for patients: reducing inequalities in health and improving services for older people in Ellerton, and shifting care closer to home in Glicestershire PCT.

- Despite a commitment to commissioning interventions that would reduce health inequalities, few specific propositions emerged. Although the independent sector and the Glicestershire Health Social Enterprise Unit made a concerted effort to promote wellness services, there appeared to be little real interest in buying these services. Most of the time was spent in discussion with acute services.

- An early development in Glicestershire was that the PCT made attempts to bring the PCO (set up to take forward commissioning) into a closer working relationship with the PCT. Surprisingly, this was well received by the PCO as it felt that through working with the PCT the PCO would have greater influence.

- In Ellerton the locality manager led many of the commissioning negotiations but was unable to deliver the follow-through support from GP colleagues.

- The Glistening PCO continued to demonstrate ambitious ideas; however, health care providers considered these ideas to be naïve concerning the potential risks involved in some of the proposals, and were therefore less willing to enter into detailed negotiations.

- By the end of 2008, despite a great deal of effort involved in developing strategies and negotiating on health service configurations, neither PCT had demonstrated significant achievements through commissioning. Both PCTs were keen to build consensus about changes with all parties. To some providers it felt that consensus was used as an elaborate way of 'risk sharing', which would not expose the PCTs as the real decision-makers or initiators of change. Providers who sought to short circuit this process by bringing all the commissioners and providers together to discuss changes to health services, based on the principle of clinical networks, were not taken seriously. Not only was gaining consensus the key priority but it also had to be delivered by the PCT controlling relationships on a bilateral basis.

- Commissioners made little attempt to use the available plurality of provision within the county to improve care for patients and appeared to be relatively resistant to any increase in independent sector involvement. This manifested itself in two ways. First, there was a real lack of decisiveness to enter into contracts with the independent sector. Even when approached with bids for new service developments that would improve patient outcomes and deliver productivity gains, the message independent sector providers received was that this was 'a good basis for discussion'. Frustrated at this response, Glicestershire PCT was asked directly whether it would encourage competition and plurality. The answer 'Yes' came with the rider 'where it could improve quality and did not interfere with sustainable services'.

- At an early stage, Ellerton PCT attempted to put its provider services on more of an arm's length basis. However, with these services referring to the arrangement as a 'devolved budget', there appeared to be little willingness to take the next step in commissioning community health services. By contrast the Glicestershire PCT providers spent most of their time finding suitable partners that would allow them to progress to becoming a community foundation trust.

- Windmill 2007 did not offer the commercial providers of commissioning services much cause for celebration in 2008. Unify Health International found it difficult to explain its commissioning offer. The SHA made it clear that it was PCTs that needed to take the lead in procuring independent sector support for commissioning. Where discussions did take place, PCTs were looking for deals that would be funded from savings achieved on commissioning budgets and for short-term consultancy assignments, rather than long-term support on commissioning. Unify's conclusions were that PCTs still needed to understand the benefits and the financial realities of contracting with the independent sector.

Improving health and social care for patients

- Overall, health care providers, as well as commissioners, concentrated on establishing and agreeing their service strategies and configurations at the expense of delivering qualitative improvements for patients. The county council's adult services had a clearer focus on delivering quality improvements, but ultimately found securing joint commissioning approaches with the NHS difficult to deliver, particularly relating to social care services. It shared the independent sector's frustration at the lack of decisiveness. It felt its own approach to commissioning was more commercial and more outcome focused.

- Glicestershire Hospitals NHS Foundation Trust had a major programme of work in reconfiguring unscheduled care and differentiating services across its two sites. It rapidly gained agreement from its membership and then proceeded to 'sell' the concept to GPs and primary care. Practice-based commissioners were treated as 'groups to convince' rather than 'groups to consult'.

- Glicestershire Hospitals NHS Foundation Trust, like St Gerald's University Hospital NHS Trust, had significant time pressures for delivering the changes in services. Both, however, found it difficult to get quick decisions from the PCT and found that the burden of public consultation hampered their ability to deliver the scale of changes needed to deliver their financial targets. They concluded that commissioning had the potential to make a real difference to their financial performance but this was more likely to be as a result of lack of planning and decision-making than having clear plans and a tough stance on negotiation.

■ St Gerald's plans had included reducing some of its elective capacity as part of a wider plan to decentralise services. However, the trust was heavily scrutinised by the SHA and Ellerton PCT, which were concerned about the political 'noise' that these proposals were generating. St Gerald's frustration was that concerns about process and consensus were overshadowing the benefits of its service changes in terms of business and patient outcomes.

■ Stellar Healthcare NHS Trust concentrated on ways of establishing a robust business that would pass Monitor's tests of viability. Resisting the merger option, Stellar explored two other options: the establishment of clinical networks with other acute providers; and the scope for vertical integration with community services, still managed by Ellerton PCT.

Patient voice and patient choice

■ An outbreak of the hospital-acquired infection MRSA at St Gerald's prompted a special review by the Healthcare Commission. The surrounding publicity proved to be one of the few triggers in the simulation to patients exercising choice. PPP, the private provider, stood out here, being the only local provider that could claim to offer an MRSA-free hospital. PPP was willing to help, but at a price. Keen to capitalise on its opportunity to gain a longer-term commitment from the PCT, PPP demanded that it was on the front page of the choice menu as the 'quid pro quo' of providing short-term capacity.

- Alongside this development we saw the early signs of a 'media war' between PPP and St Gerald's: both were eager to seize the opportunity to influence the public through the press and, in the case of PPP, through direct marketing.

- Health care providers in the simulation adopted different tactics for engaging the public and patients. Glicestershire Hospitals NHS Foundation Trust, for example, focused internally on its membership and ignored overtures from the public and patient groups. The PCTs had little time for the patient and public groups. St Gerald's preferred to use the media rather than direct relationships as a communication vehicle. Patient and public representatives found a more responsive ear in the overview and scrutiny committee and county council. All parties, however, acknowledged that they heard mixed messages, depending on which patient group or representative they talked to. The lack of consensus weakened the impact of the patient voice.

- The year started with a petition from patient groups raising concerns about the quality of older people's services in Glicestershire, which were largely run by the Social Enterprise Unit. Despite their claimed focus on social outcomes, the unit made little attempt to engage with the patient groups that had led the petition or to engage them in service redesign.

- For their part the patient and public groups found it difficult to understand the complex proposals for unscheduled care being presented by different providers. They had concerns that their involvement in service planning appeared to be focused on persuading them to support proposals that had already been developed, with little interest from commissioners and providers about addressing patient interests and preferences.

- As the year progressed, the focus on older people's services that had been triggered by patient concerns appeared to drift off the agenda of some organisations. Despite using the media to try to keep the issue in the public eye, patient groups found it difficult to understand how their concerns were being addressed and why topical issues appeared to increase and decrease in popularity with little follow-through.

■ Although this was the first round of free patient choice, providers made little attempt to market their services to GPs and to patients. Glicestershire Hospitals NHS Foundation Trust, however, did consider making car parking free.

The overview and scrutiny process

■ Faced with a number of proposals ranging from service reconfiguration between sites to the threat of a hospital closure in the centre of Ellerton, the overview and scrutiny committee proved remarkably compliant, with only the hint of an appeal to the Secretary of State for Health. The DH stance that it would not intervene in issues of service reconfiguration left the OSC with few effective levers for change. The OSC found that health service changes were poorly presented to politicians and the public even if there was a clear logic for their implementation. Clearer statements about the benefits that changes would bring for patients would help to gain OSC support. A second comment was the lack of appreciation that the NHS had for political circumstances in which local authorities operate; in particular the interface between the central political parties and local members tended to be overlooked.

Independent sector involvement

■ The two private health care providers – Amalgam, which operated a treatment centre and GP out-of-hours service, and PPP, a traditional private provider with a private hospital in the county and a newly acquired mobile health facilities business – experienced similar frustrations in their dealings with the NHS. As the Chief Executive of Amalgam commented: 'We had lots of conversations but no significant deals – it was difficult to know who actually had the authority to make decisions.'

- Amalgam held on to its contract to provide an out-of-hours GP service but, in return, Ellerton GPs demanded an agreement that Amalgam would not take over any local practices or try to establish new GP services in the area. This was a clear attempt to limit primary care competition.

- PPP, which had a healthy private sector business, questioned its continuing business with the NHS. It resented being used as a short-term 'quick fix' rather than as a serious long-term provider of quality health care. Also, ideas that it offered to prevent health and mobility problems in older people received 'short shrift'. However, it was the negotiation with Ellerton PCT over the listing on the 'choose-and-book' menus that proved the main area of concern for PPP. It argued that it would be difficult to operate in a market system where others were effectively controlling the information on its service offerings.

- By contrast the national pharmacy chain Chemico found it easier to position itself as the 'acceptable face of the private sector'. Glistening PCO commissioned a range of services from the chain, including screening, medicines management and men's health.

- The Glicestershire Health Social Enterprise Unit spent a considerable amount of time explaining the principles of social enterprise and raising concerns about the way in which it had been established. This may have been an artefact of the simulation but it is clear that there are dangers in simply transferring existing PCT provider services, without alteration, into new governance arrangements. By the end of the year the social enterprise had downsized significantly by transferring staff and rethinking its core business. There was a considerable amount of interest from the primary care commissioning groups in taking over the community nursing services in order to run these as a more integrated service with practice nursing.

- The overall conclusions from the independent sector in 2008/9, however, focused on disappointment with the difficulties in getting PCTs to make swift decisions, a lack of clarity about who was in charge of making improvements to health and health care, and concerns about whether commissioners were serious about opening up health services to greater contestability and competition.

Round two: 2010/11
The context

With the challenges, successes and disappointments from 2008/9 still relatively fresh in their minds, the Windmill 2007 players faced some significant changes to the NHS in 2010/11. The push from the centre to see greater competition and contestability demonstrated in practice was perhaps the most important development. Free-market entry for elective care and primary medical care services was to be allowed in all PCTs unless they had agreed any exemptions with the SHA. A second development was the severe resource constraints in the system, ratcheted up by the simulation moderators during the year in order to encourage participants to take them more seriously. The third major change was the new role for Monitor as the NHS 'bondholder'.

Wider developments were as follows.

- The Labour government, which had returned after the general election with a much-reduced majority, had established three key priorities for the NHS:
  - demonstrating impartial commissioning that is clearly focused on the needs of patients
  - increasing competition and choice in primary care
  - establishing free-market entry for the provision of health care.

- With the tight financial settlement for the year, all health care bodies were expected to demonstrate productivity improvements.

- Health inequalities were widening and it was recognised that they were linked to economic prosperity. PCTs and local partners were required to agree Investment for Health plans that link health, economic and environmental outcomes.

- All trusts were now foundation trusts and PCTs had only a few months to establish alternative arrangements for any provider services they may have retained. In recognition of this, PCTs were renamed local health commissioning trusts (LHCTs). Their governance also changed to mirror that of foundation trusts: they now have a board of governors and a council of members.

- There were increasing requirements on health and social care commissioners to develop joined-up solutions and greater flexibility in the use of health monies to fund social care.

- The requirement on health bodies to involve the public in planning health care (section 14) was repealed. The duty to notify and consult with overview and scrutiny committees on significant changes to services was retained.

- Monitor had a new role as bondholder for the NHS. This included overseeing capital allocations, providing low-interest loans at a similar level to the open market and ensuring that health care bodies generated an appropriate return on their assets.

- As well as these generic developments, each of the health care bodies in the simulation had a set of specific pressures to which they were asked to respond; some of these were developments that had emerged during the 2008/9 round.

Centre–local relations

- The DH had even less contact with the Central SHA/Glicestershire health system than in 2008/9. The new Independent NHS Board handled many of the enquiries and concerns raised locally. Not surprisingly the board received some heavy lobbying from different players that felt aggrieved that the system was not working in their best interests; private sector providers also made allegations of unfair competition. The Independent Board resisted most invitations to get involved. Players expected that in reality such a body would take a more interventionist line.

- The DH and SHA discussed whether there needed to be any further 'rules of engagement' to encourage greater competition in the health system. The DH was concerned that in the Central area commissioners had not fully used the benefits of competition, preferring the lever of contestability. Their emphasis had been on allowing competition for a market rather than allowing competition and plurality within a market. Although the DH felt that there were limited benefits to be gained from replacing one form of state monopoly with another, it recognised that this would not necessarily be achieved by producing a rulebook.

- The financial pressures on PCTs led to commissioning prospectuses that documented very different approaches to exclusions, restrictions and priorities. The DH was nervous about the potential challenge to the 'N' in the NHS, raising questions about whether the key issue of what the NHS should or should not fund needed to be addressed at a national level, with local decisions focusing on questions about how that range of services should be provided.

- The SHA mainly focused on managing through PCTs to achieve central targets and financial balance. By its own admission, the focus on health and inequalities received little attention, despite being a national priority.

Health care regulation and market management

- With free-market entry for elective and primary care services, and with all trusts now foundation trusts, the SHA felt it was effectively 'blind' to developments on the provider side.

- While the PCT claimed that no providers were excluded from operating a service in their area, the SHA was not convinced that the PCTs had a clear sense of what providers were doing, including the various deals that were emerging between them. Nor did the SHA feel that the PCT was actively encouraging health care providers to enter the market for primary medical and elective services. There appeared to be little, if any, management of the market in Glistershire in 2010/11.

- At this stage in the process, the PCT felt that its role and that of the SHA was becoming increasingly blurred, raising questions about whether both levels of management are needed in a truly open market system. As the PCT moved into the area of market management (albeit not particularly effectively), the authority and influence of the SHA appeared to wane.

- Monitor was busy and proactive. It paid increasingly close interest to the strategic and financial positions of the trusts. Most of its attention focused on St Gerald's University Hospitals NHS Foundation Trust, which had continued to suffer difficulties in financial performance, despite some overall improvement in the position. Although the debt recovery plans were well advanced, involving the sale of surplus land and buildings, the trust had not moved quickly enough to gain support from Monitor, which had a primary objective to ensure that there was a return on the assets in the short as well as the longer term. As a consequence Monitor made proactive moves to encourage bids to take on the management of St Gerald's.

- Monitor's enquiries stimulated a bid from the Amalgam Plc ISTC. Amalgam's values, business ethos and proposals around engaging with clinicians gave it the advantage and Monitor approved the management takeover. An alternative bid was received from PPP, which would also have been suitable. However, the relationship that Monitor had built up with Amalgam proved to be the decisive factor and it was awarded a two-year contract with a one-year notice period.

- In reality it is likely that this process would have taken longer and would have met with greater resistance from within the trust (a judicial review had been threatened but was rather overshadowed by Monitor's intervention) and possibly from its external partners. However, Monitor's requirements, decisiveness and proposed actions were felt to be realistic.

- The Healthcare Commission had made concerted efforts to keep the licensing process as simple as possible, particularly for new entrants and those needing to be re-registered as a result of mergers or changes in governance. In keeping with the commitment to reduce the burden of regulation, the Healthcare Commission offered inspection 'holidays' to organisations with consistently high performance. While the relationship with Monitor was positive, information-sharing was inconsistent.

- The Healthcare Commission's profile in 2010/11 was relatively low key. Reflecting on this, its members felt that the Commission would have a greater impact by providing information to the public to inform choice of services. How this would work in practice with increasing movement into and out of local markets, and with less central prescription of targets and standards, was felt to be a considerable challenge. With the registration process largely relating to organisations, the Commission started to reconsider the type of information it should be offering to inform patient choice around individual services.

Commissioning a patient-led NHS?

- Facing significant financial pressures, Glicestershire PCT's commissioning prospectus focused on excluding people who could not benefit from NHS health care interventions. At best this could be interpreted as a focus on improving health outcomes: at worst this tactic could have widened health inequalities by excluding the sickest and most vulnerable patients. Whatever the motivation the prospectus read as a statement of rationing rather than value for money from the health spend.

- The two PCTs had agreed to merge and downsize, with more of their commissioning responsibilities devolved to practice-based commissioning organisations. With a mandate to commission for quality and outcomes through the market, the PCT felt that this enabled it to become more strategic, focusing on assuring the quality of care delivered to patients. Unfortunately the strategic focus did not make them any more decisive in their dealings with the independent sector.

- The focus on health improvement was far less positive. The PCT largely ignored its requirement to develop Investment for Health plans with its local authority colleagues and remained primarily focused on health services and joint commissioning.

- While the PCT encouraged the PCOs to tender for services in the lower quartile of service quality, it found itself with few levers for managing the performance of practice-based commissioners, particularly relating to decisions in favour of primary care-provided services. The PCT, however, declared that it was not concerned about the dual role of primary care as commissioners and providers, as long as patients received good-quality care.

- The financial pressure on the PCT forced agreements with adult social care on joint commissioning. An interesting development, however, was that these negotiations had taken place without any involvement of the primary care commissioners.

- The financial incentives offered by tariffs proved somewhat inflexible in promoting improved health and reduced hospital admissions, and came under pressure as different players tried to manipulate the system by offering incentives to encourage less or different activity, where appropriate. For example, the Glicestershire Hospitals NHS Foundation Trust and its new acquisition, Stellar Healthcare, secured agreement from the PCT that they could share in the financial gains from reductions in emergency care as a result of the preventive model that the new trust was putting together.

Practice-based commissioning

■ The commissioning group in Ellerton continued to work with the PCT provider arm and formed a new limited company, Ellerton Health Improvement Limited, which took over the two LIFT premises. The group had to resolve how to handle poor performance in some practices, which the PCT had highlighted. Its solution was for the GPs and other staff to own the company, and the company, in turn, would employ them. The company envisaged that, while it would be unlikely to make significantly more money than currently, it would offer a stable organisational platform for the future. However, the founders were already starting to ask whether it would be possible to sell the company, which raised interesting questions about the ownership of the assets.

■ For the Glistening PCO the major success was getting the PCT to agree a wholly delegated budget for commissioning. The PCO felt this gave it greater credibility in negotiating with providers and was an important incentive for focusing on health improvement. An early deal with the Glistershire NHS Hospitals Foundation Trust provided open access to diagnostics at a price below tariff.

■ A second development was a joint venture – Integrated Health – with Unify, the independent provider of commissioning services. With Unify's help, Integrated Health introduced more systematised patterns of care with a choice of pathways for patients. This systematisation helped in improving the quality of patient care. Unify's interest in this venture was that the model was capable of replication in other parts of the country and would provide a sound platform from which to bid for primary care contracts. Integrated Health used Unify's actuarial skills to understand and plan for patient health risks, prompting a greater focus on preventive measures to improve the health of the registered population. Fast access to diagnostics was seen as an important development.

■ Integrated Health took a different approach to Ellerton to tackling poor performance, using a combination of practice takeovers, mentoring and peer support. In return for helping their peers, the supporting practices would take a share of the financial benefits of quality improvement

■ While the PCT was keen to encourage greater contestability in primary care, there was little interest in providing primary medical services from non-traditional suppliers. Even Integrated Health was reluctant to expand further into Glicestershire as it felt that having a local monopoly would be discouraged. Instead they drew on Unify's financial backing to bid for contracts in neighbouring PCTs. As this model started to develop, a further alliance with Chemico was forged. Both partnerships illustrated a trend toward larger primary care businesses being able to achieve scale economies and efficiencies through greater standardisation and supply-chain integration.

Improving health and social care for patients

■ St Gerald's University Hospitals NHS Trust made maximum use of its freedom to advertise its services and used all of its weight as a teaching hospital, resulting in significant influence over the local media.

■ The Glicestershire Health Social Enterprise Unit felt largely excluded from negotiations with the NHS because 'we didn't have enough noughts behind us', a reference to the small size and valuation of the organisation. Stirling efforts were made to shift from a focus on sickness to prevention and health improvement;

however, the unit acknowledged this required a major divestment of staff and a completely new skill mix, with greater reliance on cheaper, unqualified staff. The unit had inherited the NHS terms and conditions: therefore this shift would not be easy to achieve.

■ By contrast the unit found a more receptive purchaser in adult social care services and individual service users opting for individualised budgets. The unit stressed that its model enabled flexible, creative and responsive solutions to patients. In conclusion, while the impact on individuals would have been significant, the overall profile of social enterprise – and awareness of the contribution that it could make – remained less positive. The unit needed larger partners that could invest in the organisation and help to replicate the model on a larger scale.

■ Stellar Healthcare, having reviewed its strategy of clinical networking and decentralising services, concluded that it did not have a sustainable future, given its size and remit and the challenges in raising sufficient funds to facilitate the transition to a new business model. Its emergency services in particular did not have a sufficient catchment to be viable in the longer term. An alliance with Ellerton PCT's provider services enabled the two parties to refocus attention on preventing hospital admissions. While a move toward vertical integration in governance would have been a sensible option to underpin these changes, Ellerton community services was determined to form a community foundation trust, and the leaders at Stellar proved reluctant to give up all hospital services. Eventually, the alternative option – a merger with the Glicestershire Hospitals NHS Foundation Trust – had greater appeal to the Stellar management team.

■ Negotiations between Stellar and Glicestershire Hospitals NHS Foundation Trust took place without any reference to the SHA and, seemingly, the PCT. These discussions were handled entirely by the two trusts and Monitor. Monitor's focus was on ensuring that the merger made economic sense and that there was sufficient cultural alignment between the two organisations for the merger to work in practice and to deliver the promised benefits quickly.

■ The incentive for Glicestershire Hospitals NHS Foundation Trust in entering into this deal was twofold. First, the proposals helped with its reconfiguration and decentralisation plans; second, the trust had generated significant surpluses, which it would lose if they were not reinvested in health service improvements or developments. The trust had generated for reinvestment in health services: that is, it had to 'spend it or lose it'.

Patient voice and patient choice

■ The PCT largely ignored its new 'members', preferring to use surveys, polls, citizens' juries and similar methods to get an informed view of public and patient opinion. Some tokenistic consultation on the preparation of the commissioning prospectus had taken place, but the patient representatives felt that this had been entirely focused on rationing decisions.

■ In contrast with their treatment by the PCT, patient groups felt that the true power lay with the trusts, although these bodies did not invite their views to any significant degree. The active patient groups moved into campaigning mode, lobbying the OSC and courting the media as a way of getting their voices heard.

■ Throughout 2010/11, as providers took forward a range of partnerships and plans, patients found it difficult to understand what was happening and what services were available. The lack of engagement with the PCT meant that patients struggled to find a neutral guide who could inform them of the available service and treatment options to enable them to exercise choices effectively.

The overview and scrutiny process

■ In 2010/11 the OSC bowed to the pressure from individual patient groups and recognised that it was hearing different views depending on whom it spoke to. However, it did share a common concern with the patient groups about the way in which the commissioning prospectus had been presented.

■ The local authority was facing similar financial pressures to those in the health sector. This led the OSC to focus more on the impact that the prospectus might have on the adult social care budget than on the expectation of widening health inequalities.

Independent sector involvement

■ PPP continued to experience frustration with its dealings with the NHS, which were compounded by developments taking place in vertical integration, and antagonism from patient representatives about the involvement of the private sector in delivering care to the NHS. PPP concluded that very little movement in referrals would happen and that patient choice would have limited impact on its business. Paradoxically Glicestershire PCT's commissioning prospectus provided the catalyst for new business development. In response to the significant financial pressures, the prospectus introduced a range of exclusions from NHS funding for patient groups and interventions unlikely to deliver any material health gains. PPP then saw this as an opportunity to withdraw completely from NHS work.

■ PPP felt liberated from its negotiations with the NHS and concentrated on running its business. It invested its new energy and creativity in exploiting the potential for private work for individuals excluded by the NHS's funding regime. Unify Health International was contracted to undertake the actuarial work to quantify demand and risk. Armed with this information PPP started to target people in the lower interest groups, offered interest-free loans for health care treatments and negotiated a contract with the local authority to provide lifestyle and direct referral services.

- PPP also exploited the uncertainty at St Gerald's and the over-supply of doctors by offering St Gerald's medical staff attractive rates. It was able to set the tone in the newly emerging medical workforce market.

- Amalgam's fate, as indicated earlier, was ultimately different to that of PPP, although it did almost withdraw from dealings with the NHS. Its investors had given it a clear budget and timescale within which to deliver returns on its upfront investment. With continuing delays in decision-making by trusts and PCTs about Amalgam's propositions, there was a sense that the NHS did not count the cost of negotiation and decision-making, whereas for private sector colleagues this is a period of high risk.

Concluding observations

In 2008/9 the Glicestershire health community struggled to utilise the full range of levers that had been introduced in the reform of the health service. Decisions about new services or ways of working showed echoes of the older regime where achieving consensus and maintaining stability were considered the hallmarks of effective commissioning. From a health care reform perspective this appeared to be a disappointing picture – and a frustrating one for new players keen to make their mark in the delivery of services to the NHS. But for the users of health and social care services the disappointments would have been greater – this cautious approach left them with limited improvements in their health or health care.

Overall, 2010/11 saw greater dynamism in the health care provider market. On the commissioning front the role of PCTs became less clear as all health care providers had freedom to operate in the local market, if they felt it offered them attractive returns. Practice-based commissioning was successful when backed by larger bodies or where there were solutions relating to premises to enable the provider side of primary care to expand.

The health market appeared to be largely unregulated other than through performance monitoring of quality. Providers appeared to be free to make decisions and deals with whatever organisation they liked. Nevertheless, the cultural antipathy in the NHS to the independent sector appeared to continue. Even the Social Enterprise Unit, which brings a value base that could be considered to be more in line with the NHS, found it difficult to get involved in the so-called 'health market'.

With some signs of market failure starting to show, Monitor proved to be the influential player in securing the stability of the health system.

Traditional representation of the patients and public through the official organisations failed to offer what trusts and PCTs really needed to understand patient needs and preferences. The need to invest in more reliable and impartial approaches to assessing public and consumer opinion, however, was recognised as essential.

Three significant factors emerged as the drivers of innovation and improvement.

- First, partnerships and alliances between different providers and across sectors opened up new opportunities and ways of thinking about health care delivery.

- Second, it was the resource constraints that finally pushed PCT commissioning beyond delivering more of the same.

- Third, the SHA's requirement that commissioners justify exclusions to the local health market pushed competition for and within the health market to a new level.

Appendix 1: The Windmill participants

Kevin Barton, Chief Executive, Lambeth PCT
Geoff Benn, Group Marketing Director, Care UK
Paul Bennett, Director of Commissioning, Surrey PCT
Lindsey Bloomfield, Strategic Funding Manager, Roche
Sandy Briddon, Interim Network Director, South Central PCT Alliance
Mark Britnell, Chief Executive, South Central SHA
Miranda Carter, Assessment Director, Monitor
Patricia Cassidy, Commercial Director and Group Clinical Director, Nuffield
    Hospitals
Nav Chana, Associate Director for Vocational Training, London Deanery
Caroline Clarke, Director of Finance and Information, Homerton University
    Hospital NHS Foundation Trust
David Costain, Medical Director, AXA PPP Healthcare
Angela Coulter, Chief Executive, Picker Institute Europe
Michael Coupe, Director of Strategy, Royal Cornwall Hospitals NHS Trust
Anna Dixon, Deputy Director of Policy, King's Fund
Jennifer Dixon, Director of Policy, King's Fund
Michelle Dixon, Director of Communications, King's Fund
Ian Dodge, Policy Strategy Directorate, Department of Health
Andrew Eyres, Director of Finance and Information, Lambeth PCT
Simon Fradd, Co-founder, Concordia Health
Mo Girach, Independent Consultant
Neil Griffiths, Hospital Director, University College London Hospitals NHS
    Foundation Trust
Stephen Hay, Chief Operating Officer, Monitor
Nick Hicks, Director of Public Health, Milton Keynes PCT
Matthew James, Commercial Manager, Nuffield Hospitals
Miranda Kavanagh, Head of Communications and Engagement, Healthcare
    Commission
Ron Kerr, Chief Executive, United Bristol Healthcare NHS Trust
Gary King, Managing Director, Vanguard Healthcare Solutions, Nuffield
    Hospitals

Kate Lobley, Head of Operations, Healthcare Commission
Kay Mackay, Director of Strategic Development and Innovation, Surrey PCT
Charlie MacNally, Head of Adult Services, Bedfordshire County Council
Jonathan Marron, Policy Director, Monitor
Jonathan Marshall, GP, Wendover Health Centre
Adrian Masters, Director of Strategy, Monitor
Ben May, Administrative Assistant, King's Fund
Kaye McIntosh, Freelance Journalist,
John McIvor, Chief Executive, Lincolnshire PCT
Elaine McNichol, Director of Enterprise and Innovation, Centre for the
    Development of Healthcare Policy and Practice
David Mobbs, Chief Executive, Nuffield Hospitals
Gwyn Morris, Head of Older People's Services, Royal Borough of Kensington
    and Chelsea
James Morris, Senior Researcher, Opinion Leader Research
David Moses, Head of Scrutiny, Hertfordshire County Council
John Offord, Director of Finance and Performance, Cambridgeshire PCT
Paul O'Hanlon, Director of Clinical Commercials, Lloyds Pharmacy
Jo O'Rourke, Keynote Events Consulting
Sam Ours, Chief Administrative Officer, United Healthcare Europe
Jane Pilkington, Associate Director of Public Health, Stockport PCT
Stephen Ramsden, Chief Executive, Luton and Dunstable Hospital Trust
Jamie Rentoul, Head of Strategy, Healthcare Commission
Daniel Reynolds, Head of Press and Public Affairs, King's Fund
Tim Richardson, GP Epsom, Surrey
Bob Ricketts, Director of Demand Side Reform, Department of Health
Ty Robinson, Managing Director, Navigant Consulting
Heather Rogers, Director of Healthcare Public Affairs Practice, Edelman UK
Ann Smart, Project Director, Service Reconfiguration, Barking and Dagenham
    PCT
Janice Steed, Director of Strategic Development and Commissioning,
    Cambridgeshire PCT
Barbara Walsh, Director, Change Through Partnership
Katherine Ward, Director of Commissioning, United Healthcare Europe
John Webster, Director of Performance and Information, E&N Hertfordshire
    NHS Trust
Paul Whiteside, Chief Executive, UK Specialist Hospitals Ltd
David Williams, Director of Services, Ealing PCT

Simulation moderators

Niall Dickson, Chief Executive, King's Fund
Caro Millington, Former Chair, North West London SHA
Bill Moyes, Executive Chairman, Monitor

Windmill design team

John Appleby, Chief Economist, King's Fund
Sarah Harvey, Director, Loop2
Alasdair Liddell, Senior Associate, King's Fund
Laurie McMahon, Director, Loop2

Appendix 2: The Windmill commentators

Advisory group

Nicky Agelopoulos, Marie Curie

Jan Aps, Head of Health Strategy and Development, Audit Commission

Kevin Barton, Chief Executive, Lambeth PCT

Carol Black, National Director for Health and Work, Department of Work and Pensions

Andrew Cash, Director General for Provider Development at the Department of Health

Patricia Cassidy, Commercial Director and Group Clinical Director, Nuffield Hospitals

Howard Catton, Head of Policy Development and Implementation, Royal College of Nursing

Will Cavendish, Head of Strategy, Policy and Strategy Directorate, Department of Health

Cyril Chantler, Chairman, King's Fund

Caroline Clarke, Director of Finance, Homerton University Hospital NHS Foundation Trust

Paul Corrigan, Director of Strategy and Commissioning, NHS London

Kolade Daodu, on behalf of Sabina Khan, Social Enterprise London

Richard Davidson, Cancer Research UK

Niall Dickson, Chief Executive, King's Fund

Karen Didovich, Independent Sector Employment Relations, Royal College of Nursing

Anna Dixon, Deputy Director of Policy, King's Fund

Michelle Dixon, Director of Communications, King's Fund

Adrian Eddleston, Vice Chair, King's Fund

Mark Goldman, Chief Executive, Heart of England NHS Foundation Trust

Stephen Hay, Chief Operating Officer, Monitor

Philip Hurst, Policy Manager Health and Social Care, Age Concern

Julie Jones, Immediate Past President, ADSS

Malcolm Lowe Lauri, Chief Executive, King's College Hospital NHS Trust

Kay Mackay, Director of Strategic Development and Innovation, Surrey PCT
Caro Millington, Former Chair, North West London SHA
David Mobbs, Chief Executive, Nuffield Hospitals
Bill Moyes, Executive Chairman, Monitor
Robert Naylor, Chief Executive, University College London Hospitals NHS
    Foundation Trust
Jonathan Nicholls, Head of NHS Research, Ipsos MORI
Gwen Nightingale, Senior Policy Researcher, Health, Audit Commission
Sean O'Sullivan, Senior Policy Analyst, Royal College of Midwives
Alpesh Patel, Partner, Head of Healthcare, Ernst and Young
Ty Robinson, Managing Director, Navigant Consulting
Alastair Scotland, Executive Director, National Patient Safety Agency
Sue Slipman, Director, FT Network
Michael Sobanja, Chief Executive, NHS Alliance
Kevin Smith, Navigant Consulting
Mark Smith, Group Strategy Director, Mercury
Richard Smith, Chief Executive, UnitedHealth Europe
Tom Smith, Senior Policy Analyst, BMA
Matthew Swindells, Policy Adviser to the Secretary of State for Health,
    Department of Health
Maxine Taylor, Director of Policy and Communications, Cancer Research UK
Sarah Thewlis, Chief Executive and Registrar, Nursing and Midwifery Council
Nick Timmins, Public Policy Editor, Financial Times
Jo Webber, Deputy Policy Director, NHS Confederation
Alison Wetherall, Head of Healthcare, Macmillan Cancer Support
Melba Wilson, Acting Chief Executive, London Development Centre
Julie Wood, NHS Alliance